HABIT TRIGGERS

HOW TO CREATE BETTER ROUTINES AND SUCCESS
RITUALS

TO MAKE LASTING CHANGES IN YOUR LIFE

ROMUALD ANDRADE

Habit Triggers . 2

Contents

YOUR FREE GIFT

As a way of saying, "Thanks for your purchase," I'm offering a free download of my ebook "Wake Up Successful - How to Increase Your Energy & Achieve Any Goal with a Morning Routine".

Getting Unstuck is a real problem for a lot of people. The trick is to identify what you need to get done and create a step-by-step strategy to launch your day so that you execute your tasks in the most efficient way possible.

In "Wake Up Successful" you'll discover several ways to launch your day with a tried and tested morning routine. This will enable you to make lasting changes to your work, success, health and sleep habits.

You can download this free ebook by clicking here

http://7bigrocks.com/mr/

http://7bigrocks.com/mr/

WILL THIS BOOK HELP ME?

You are probably reading this book because:

-   You find it difficult to break the negative habits that have been holding you back.
-   You have tried to use willpower — and failed…multiple times. Sooner or later, you drop the new diet or quit the gym or go on a shopping frenzy.
-   You want to create positive financial habits and make lasting changes in your life.
-   You have tasted temporary success but failed to make lasting changes.
-   You want to make changes to your unhealthy lifestyle by practicing simple daily habits.
-   You need practical steps to develop better habits.

A lot of the elements in this book are intuitive, and you may already know some or all of them. The methods I suggest in this book are gathered from people much smarter than me. All I have done is try each one out and testis to examine what works and what does not.

The easy-to-understand system that has resulted from my efforts is something I am proud of, but I am not writing this book to be preachy. You're smart enough to know that there are no "secrets" in life. Most people intuitively know that "exercising is good!" but what they don't realize is that exercising affects other areas of life and causes a chain reaction.

Creating a healthy exercise routine is not really about willpower. I will show you how you can use the triggers that are part of your daily life to help you make massive changes in your life and take you from "knowing" to "doing."

When I began to write this book, I simply wrote out the trigger system with a few examples and thought I was done. However, after reading the draft a few times, I realized that I had made some critical assumptions about you. The reason these assumptions are critical is because if they happen to be wrong, then this whole book would be rendered useless. I have listed out my assumptions below to ensure that we are on the same page:

#1. I assume you are reading this book because there is an element in your life that seems to be out of control. It may be your body weight, your mental state, or the state of your finances.

#2. I also assume that you have identified the problem and that you are willing to do whatever it takes to rip this problem apart.

#3. I assume that you can take the framework suggested and run with it; that is, you would be able to customize the framework to fit your life.

#4. While outlining the trigger system, I will also assume that you are willing to suspend judgment and give this system a chance.

I would like to believe that I can help you solve this problem, but I struggle with the fact that I don't know you and I don't know the exact problems you are facing. I also don't know if my method will fit your life. But you can rest assured for two reasons:

1. You won't have to start this journey alone. I have created a website, www.7bigrocks.com, where you will have access to additional information, templates, and free downloads to help take this forward.

2. You can always reach out to me by sending me an email. My email address is 7bigrocks@gmail.com.

INTRODUCTION

Men's natures are alike;
It is their habits that separate them.
~Confucius

Everyone has both good and bad habits. Good habits can be hard to form, while bad ones can be hard to break. However, if you understand how habits actually work, then you can make them work for you.

Charles Duhigg, a writer, talks about three different aspects involved in creating a habit. He calls them the *cue*, the *routine*, and the *reward*.

The cue is what triggers your brain.
The routine may be a mental routine, a physical routine, or an emotional routine.
The reward helps the brain to decide whether or not that habit is worth remembering.

Your brain is led by your habits. Your habits could be financial habits, behavioral habits, health related habits, thinking habits, emotional habits, shopping habits, business habits, or location-based habits.

Habits create patterns that we regularly follow until doing so feels almost involuntary. However, a lot of people think that habits and addictions are similar in nature. The reason for that is the fact that bad habits and addictions have a lot in common. Let us examine this further.

Habits vs. Addictions

The term *habit* refers to a behavior pattern repeated to the point where the brain does it automatically. An addiction, on the other hand, refers to the body's compulsive need for particular substances or things that, if denied, leads to some horrible effects. While a habit can be controlled or even modified, an addiction is beyond the control of the person affected and can only be modified if one receives the help of a professional.

Distinguishing between habits and addictions is not as straightforward as it may sound. One of the more effective approaches in differentiating between the two is to look at the outcomes of the behavior in question. Ask yourself, "What are the long-term effects of this behavior? Are they disruptive and negative, or essentially balanced and positive?"

In addition, to this, you can get useful insights if you examine whether or not you are able to maintain a conscious choice before you act out the behavior: Does the behavior compel your brain to indulge, or is it your brain that independently opts to act as you do? The following is a list of some significant though often subtle differences between habits and addictions:

<u>A (Good) Habit is a Behavior Pattern that:</u>
#1. Is repeated constantly to the point where it becomes second nature
#2. Is developed after repeated (or practiced) exposure, usually after making conscious choice
#3. Manifests itself through regularity
#4. Over time leads to accuracy of performance or increase in output
#5. Allows you to make a conscious and straightforward choice
#6. Over time leads to outcomes which are balanced and beneficial to yourself as well as to others

<u>An Addiction is a Behavior Pattern that:</u>
#1. Has run out of control and made you a slave to it
#2. Is developed either through initiation to something or exposure to a substance that gives an incentive and reward to the body. The reward or incentive may be in the form of stored memories, or *cues*, which remind the brain of the rewarding experience after indulging in the behavior pattern.
#3. Appears with even more regularity over time
#4. Leads to decreased facility and performance accuracy over time
#5. Gradually diminishes the possibility of a conscious, straightforward choice
#6. Leads to long-term effects that are negative (the bad outweighs the good) both to self and others. These outcomes are also typically unbalanced.

You may notice that, for the purposes of this book, I am focusing on how to create good habits and eliminate bad habits. However, if the bad habit has grown to the point where it has become an addiction, this book may not be the right way to go, and you might need to consult a professional or check into rehab.

The Importance of Cultivating the Right Habits

I am firmly convinced that habits are the most defining of all human traits. Habits are by far the most trustworthy indicators of who we are and our destinies. The significance of habits in this sense even exceeds the role played by such concepts as our beliefs and thoughts.

When you come to think of it, unless we work on our thoughts and beliefs, just having them is for all intents and purposes worthless. Thoughts and beliefs are only worth having if they spur us to act accordingly. It is only when we act on our beliefs and thoughts that we give any sort of meaning to them.

If you want to know what someone believes and how they actually think, you need only look at their actions. If there is any redeemable value attached to our character, it is to be found in the sum of our actions. And habits, being the actions we do often and repeatedly, announce to all and sundry what our beliefs truly are.

Consequently, if we are looking to do anything

life-changing with ourselves, we have to begin by learning about our habits and then working on them.

After studying many biographies and interviewing many successful people, I have come to the conclusion that most of them got there due to their habits. Admittedly, factors such as luck, genetics, talent, circumstances and type of upbringing all contributed to these inspirational people achieving greatness, but if there is one common denominator that places all of them in one category, it is that they cultivated routines and habits that were firmly in line with their goals. They only managed to get to the top by doing things they firmly believed in, well and consistently.

This is a very inspiring realization because there is very little (if anything at all) we can do to influence factors such as genetics, luck, circumstances, upbringing or talents. But when it comes to habits, this is where we are fully in control, making their importance such a monumental factor in determining our success or failure.

But so many of us have tried to form and maintain the right habits, and more often than not we tend to fail. It does not matter whether we resolve to commit to an effective fitness regimen, eat healthier food, or lead happier lives — achieving consistency is always such a steep hill to climb. Is it possible to do anything about this, though?

In the next chapter, we will examine the reasons why we are unable to maintain lifestyle changes consistently.

CHANGING BEHAVIOR AND POOR LIFESTYLE HABITS.

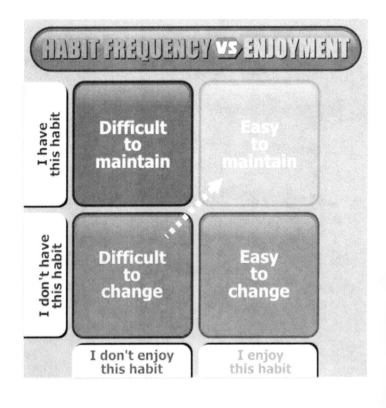

A large number of people have unhealthy habits, which can include poor diets, smoking, laziness and lack of self-control. Sometimes, we are able to identify the problem and we try to make changes. However, we fail almost the same number of times we try. It is also common for people to start off with good habits that will bring tremendous benefits to their life and practice them for a considerably long period of time, only to quit and give up.

After attending the Global Innovation Outlook Conference hosted by IBM, Adam Deutschman, the author of *Change or Die*, took notes on a number of things. One of the speakers at the event, Dr. Edward Miller, former dean of Johns Hopkins Medical School, caught his attention. His topic was patients who suffer from heart diseases. Some of his patients were so ill that they were forced to undergo bypass surgery, which can cost $100,000 or more. About 600,000 people in the United States undergo this procedure and close to 1.3 million have angioplasties. The total cost of these treatments is around $30 billion, which is a ridiculously huge amount. The procedures merely reduce chest pains and will do little towards prolonging life or preventing heart attacks.

The irony, as expressed by Dr. Miller, is that 90% of patients who undergo surgical grafting and bypass do not change their lifestyle habits. You meet a patient two years after surgery and they are still doing the same things that got them into hospital. This is the power of habit —nine out of 10 heart disease patients, who are in danger of heart attacks and even sudden death, will not change their lifestyles!

As mentioned above, change can be very difficult, and most people make resolutions that they stick to for a short while only to give up even after developing a workable, effective plan. Here are some of the most common stories that I have heard. Perhaps you can relate to some of them:

I got into the habit of waking up at 5:30 am and did that for about three months before giving up. I can barely get out of bed before 7:30 am ever since.

I started jogging three times a week and did it for about two months before giving up once again.

I made meal plans that I only followed for a short period (just four months) before I quit.

Why are lifestyle changes so difficult to hold on to?

The most obvious reason why changing is hard is simple boredom. There are many studies that clearly link the amount of enjoyment you experience from a habit to the frequency of the habit. Changes are boring to make and go contrary to our accustomed way of living. There is also the myth that it requires strong willpower to stick to a change, and the focus must always remain on why you need the change.

There are three major ways you can incorporate new habits in your life. The first is Keystone Habits, the second is Micro Habits, and the last is Habit Swapping.

KEYSTONE HABITS

We first make our habits,
and then our habits make us.
~ John Dryden

Keystone habits are very important in initiating lifestyle changes. The term originated from the architectural term "keystone," which refers in literal terms to a central stone that locks the entire building arch together. Keystone habits, therefore, are fundamental changes that act as foundations upon which even much greater changes can be initiated and developed.

These habits result in a snowball effect by influencing and creating an environment where other changes can thrive. In other words, keystone habits cause a chain reaction that influences other behaviors or actions. The end results are more willpower, less stress, better health, contentment, and many other benefits.

If you want to initiate changes that will bring about more satisfaction with life, better health, less stress, and more energy, take a look at these three keystone habits:

1. A morning routine

The reason most people aren't successful is that they fail to follow a day-by-day strategy. Instead, they start each day "hoping" they will have enough time to take action on their goals.

If you closely examined the world's most successful people, you'd see they start each day in an energized state, ready to accomplish any goal.

What's their secret?

The "one thing" they do differently is that they prioritize each day so the most important task is completed first. Put simply, successful people have morning routines that help them feel energized and ready to focus on their most important goal. In my book, *Wake Up Successful*, you'll discover several ways to launch your day with a tried and tested morning routine. This will enable you to make lasting changes to your work, success, health, and sleep habits.

You can download this book for free from here: http

2. Exercise

Regular exercises mandatory for anyone who wants to lead a healthy lifestyle. As a matter of fact, there is no such thing as a healthy or good lifestyle habit that does not incorporate exercise. The benefits of exercise range from increased heart rate to reduced anxiety, improved metabolism, increased energy levels, and greater consciousness as a result of improved brain function.

Exercising makes it possible to experience many other positive changes. It increases work productivity, reduces stress and impulsive emotions, strengthens willpower, and improves overall health. If you are looking for the best keystone habit to start inculcating into your program, then regular exercise will lead you to a better lifestyle filled with strong willpower, self control, and abundant strength.

3. A good night's sleep

Due to the current economic changes, more people are pushed to do double shifts and extra hours. Combined with the need to socialize and have some fun in your life, it is very difficult to get a good night's sleep.

It is important to acknowledge the role of sleep in your life. The mere fact that you will only last 11 days before death if you do not sleep and can last up to a month without food should explain everything. Sleep is when the body is repaired, regenerated, and rejuvenated. Without sleep, your muscles experience constant wear and tear and you will be exhausted.

Poor sleep hygiene also leads to slowed brain activity, loss of concentration, and even insanity as the habit progresses. It may lead to overdependence on drugs, which are what we are trying to run away from. On the other hand, a good night's sleep will result in improved brain function, higher energy levels, repair of muscle and cell damage, elimination of toxins, and better concentration. You will wake up strong, determined, focused and suited to handle any task that comes your way.

How can you identify your own keystone habits? You use the 7 Big Rocks Trigger System!

Step 1: Grab a pen and paper and note down your bad habits for each of the following "big rocks."

#1. Your health, food, and exercise
#2. How you start and end your workday
#3. Your urges
#4. Your unproductive activities
#5. How you manage your emotional responses
#6. How you spend your money
#7. Things you procrastinate on that you know you really should be doing

Step 2: Select one bad habit *from each* of the 7 areas mentioned above. Identify and write down the *trigger event* that leads to the bad habit for each of the 7 bad habits you have identified.

Step 3: Identify a suitable replacement behavior for the trigger event in each of the 7 areas.

Step 4: Write down the replacement behavior (habit swap) for each of the trigger events using the following format (a when-then plan)

WHEN _____ Happens, THEN I will

_____

An example:

WHEN:
- I end my workday

THEN I will:
–   Review what I accomplished today, writing down a short, bulleted summary of each accomplishment. **THEN,** I will:
–   Plan tomorrow's tasks. **THEN,** I will:
–   Place my planned tasks where I will see them first thing tomorrow.

I admit that this "when-then" plan does seem overly simplistic, and a common objection I have encountered while helping people is that they have a problem getting started with it because their lives are overly complicated, so they don't think a simple solution to nurture their good habits will work.

So the first step, according to me, would be to simplify your life by trying out the following:

- Watch less TV and read more.
- Drive less and walk more.
- Shop less and spend more time outdoors.
- Focus on the present, not so much on the past or the future.
- Avoid noise and choose solitude and quiet.
- Play more and work less.
- Don't forget to breathe, slowly and consciously.

In the next chapter, I will share my own experiences with something I call Habit Swapping.

MY OWN EXPERIENCE WITH HABIT SWAPPING

Bad habits are easier
to abandon today than tomorrow.
~Yiddish Proverb

A lot of what I say sounds "preachy," and so I would like to relate my own experience with bad habits and how I identified those triggers and used the same triggers to "install" good habits to replace the bad ones.

One of my bad habits was interrupting people in conversation. When my wife (not so) lovingly pointed out that I kept interrupting people when they were talking, my response was typical of "me."

Firstly, I thought my wife was confused. Obviously, the subject of the conversation was in my area of expertise and I was just contributing to the conversation, not interrupting the third party!

Next, it dawned on me that maybe she was not as confused as I thought she was, so I did the obvious thing — I went into denial mode. The criticism did not apply to me because I had a valid reason for adding to the conversation.

Finally, when my feeble reason failed, I tried to discredit her statement and change the topic, but the conversation remained with me and played in my mind. It was only when I started studying habit triggers that I realized I could actually use the information to change even small behaviors like these to make positive changes in my life.

In this case, the trigger for me was a topic I was passionate about. A third party was talking about a book that I really loved and was narrating their own experience. The person tried unsuccessfully to relate that experience twice, but I kept on bringing the topic back to what I wanted to talk about and kept going…yada, yada, yada.

In this case, the first part of the solution was for me to accept that there was a problem because the third party felt she could not get a word in edgewise. The second part was identifying the trigger, which in this case was a topic that I found interesting, and the third part was finding a replacement behavior — in this case, waiting for a break in the conversation and then saying something to the effect of, "I had a similar experience, but it's a bit of a long story. Would you like to hear it?"

I will put this in the form of a when-then plan for you:

WHEN:
- I am having a conversation with someone and

they bring up an interesting topic

THEN, I will:
- Listen to what they have to say about the topic.
THEN, I will:
- Ensure I do not interrupt. **THEN,** I will:
- Wait for a break in the conversation. **THEN,** I will:
- Ask for permission to tell a long story.

It might seem easy to remember this when-then plan, but I would strongly advise you to write it down and file it into a three-ring binder. Simply articulating this strategy on paper will ensure you can modify it if it does not work and will also help you structure your thought process.

Replacing your own negative behavior

Habits don't die as long as the trigger is around. This is why the best way to break a bad habit is by replacing it with a new one. The example I gave above may seem a bit simplistic, but that is the best part about habit swapping. It works regardless of whether the habit is a small one like biting your nails or a long-term habit such as smoking. It works when you keep the same trigger and a similar reward, but a different action. So, if you bite your nails, chew gum when you feel the urge to bite.

It's possible to find a suitable replacement behavior for most habits. First, find the trigger for the habit and something that can substitute for it. As an example, if you regularly swear, replace your curses with acceptable words like "darn" and "shoot." If eating a candy bar before sleeping is a habit, eat a sliced apple or a bowl of air-popped popcorn before the candy craving kicks in.

Suppose you want to start a new behavior rather than change one, like running every morning before going to work. Do this by remembering the formula: trigger, behavior, and reward. While running is the behavior, you need to create a trigger and reward to encourage the habit.

Self-created triggers are rituals performed before the behavior, like setting your running clothes and shoes near your alarm clock before sleeping. Upon waking up, seeing the clothes triggers you to work out. After doing this a few times, the endorphin rush and sense of accomplishment will soon make it a habit.

It might not be easy to replace behaviors and create new triggers. You may have to try to find out what works for you. Placing your clothes near the alarm clock might not work, as you sometimes knock them to the floor while shutting off the alarm. You may also be so tired that you directly head to the bathroom without seeing the clothes. It may therefore work better to place your clothes in the bathroom.

Remember, you will never know whether a trigger will work until you try. Test different triggers till you find the most effective one.

In the next chapter, we will learn how to crack the habit code by using Micro Habits.

THE MICRO HABIT APPROACH TO ACHIEVING SUCCESS IN LIFE

Your habits determine your destiny.
~Joel Osteen

A micro habit is a small version of a complex goal. For example, writing 5,000 words may seem like a very complicated job, but if you make a micro goal of writing 50 words every day, the task will not look so intimidating. Micro habits are too small to intimidate you into inaction, but when done consistently can help you attain monumental achievements.

B.J. Fogg wrote an article where he introduced the concept of micro habits, which he referred to as "tiny habits." Bestselling author Stephen Guise also talks about this concept in his book, where he refers to them as "mini-habits." However, the concept is the same, and I would like to acknowledge these two authors for their work.

Micro habits are clear and easily attainable goals that require very little time to accomplish. Putting in place a micro-habit strategy is an effective way to ensure tasks that appear overwhelming are made more manageable. Micro habits do not lessen the work that needs to be done; they only serve to motivate you to do enough for the day and possibly even exceed what you thought possible.

Even when you lack motivation, it is easy to finish the task at hand as it does not call for plenty of effort. Applying micro habits is a proven way to make lasting changes in your life.

These examples will serve to illustrate the effectiveness of micro habits:
To read a book in one week, read a chapter daily.
To walk a mile, begin by taking 30 steps.
To write a whole book, complete one chapter every week.
To lose weight, begin by eating a bowl of oatmeal a day.

Because micro habits help you achieve immediate success, this motivates you to go and do even better next time. Micro habits also help to get rid of the guilty feelings you have when you fail to attain a desired goal. They keep failure and the associated feelings of disappointment at bay. They train you to focus on success and make achieving success the norm rather than the exception.

Your habits are the single greatest denominator determining your character and identity. To make a life-transforming change in your life, therefore, you need to begin with setting up identity-based goals, ones based on your beliefs about who you are.

There are 3 steps necessary to achieve this transformation:

#1. **Decide the Type of Person You Want to Be:** You are creating a wholly new version of yourself, so it is necessary to be careful before making a choice. Do you want to become more popular, or richer? Would you rather be a more outgoing person with great connections with those near and far? Is your dream to appear sexier, prettier, or healthier? Whatever your dream is, the first step to achieving it is creating a clear concept of this image with clear and specific goals.

#2. **Set up Goals and Make them Powerful Habits:** To achieve your ultimate dream, begin by setting up clear-cut goals and set up the task of achieving them, one by one. This habit of constant victory will set you on your way to becoming the person you really want to be. It is very empowering to believe you can entirely transform your life, and this only happens with relentless achievement of goals.   If you want to become a healthy and physically fit person, it is obvious that you have to exercise daily. Even if you start with a 15-minute daily walk around the block, that's a great foundation to build upon, and will be easier than trying to run for two hours continuously.

#3. **Raise your Standards to Achieve Confidence:** Make a complete list of behaviors you want to change and the end results to measure this transformation. Begin by demanding excellence from yourself and start leading a life that is meaningful and goal-directed. Carefully lay down strategies that bring your preferred results. Get rid of beliefs and doubts that hold you back from being the best that you can be.

This may sound intimidating at first, but the following steps will help make it more straightforward:

Believe staunchly that success is yours for the taking, and your subconscious mind will believe this too. Your habits will automatically be focused on success.

Don't let your belief waver, even when the odds seem stacked against you. Don't take your sight off the ultimate objective. Feel the "new" you as you gradually transform.

Always act and do your tasks with consistency. Grow an aversion for half-done tasks and abandoned projects. Follow through with vigor, and more often than not, you will have your way in the end.

Here are some practical steps on how you can achieve consistency of action and make success second nature:

Wake up earlier. Keep your running shoes and tracksuit ready before you go to bed so you can begin your workout straight away.

Always have a healthy snack in the fridge so that

you can eat healthy when you have a craving.

Maintain a calendar of exercises, a list of healthy food to eat, and a list of things to do in order to save time and retain objectivity in your goals.

Create or print out some positive statements or mantras to spur you on to achieving greatness.

Choosing your MicroHabits

In a way, achieving greatness begins by conquering your mind first. There are two parts to our brain. The primitive part of our brain is primarily motivated to seek pleasure. Seth Godin refers to this as our "Lizard Brain" while others call it the "reptilian brain." While pleasure-based positive reinforcement learning does work, it is ineffective for achieving long-term goals due to our reptilian brain trying to maintain the status quo.

To overcome our pleasure-based reptilian brain, we need to include another piece to complete the puzzle: pain. Avoiding pain is the antithesis of seeking pleasure, but it works very well in achieving long-term goals using a gradual system of incrementing your attainment of objectives.

Habits can change when you achieve a perfect balance between rewards (positive reinforcement) and fear of pain (negative reinforcement). This three-step formula will help you sever off your ties to negative habits:

Step 1: Create a MicroHabit Geared to Achieving Your Big Goal

Your current behavior reflects your identity, the person you believe (consciously or subconsciously) that you are. To achieve the most complete change of behavior, you need to start by believing new things about yourself. It is therefore much more effective to set goals which are centered on your performance or appearance. Something like *"I want to lose 40 pounds"* or "*I want to run the marathon in less than three hours"*.

While performance- and appearance-based goals are great, they do not really equate to habits. These goals help if you are already practicing a behavior and are aiming to drive it forward. For purposes of starting an entirely new and desirable behavior, what you need are identity-based goals. Your identity is the beginning point of forming desirable habits. Each one of your actions has to be spurred on by the belief that being great is possible.

Achieving consistency with a new behavior or habit is usually difficult because so many of us try to achieve appearance- or performance-based goals without doing anything about our identity. It is only by renewing the sense of your identity that you can rise up from mediocrity to true greatness.

Some behaviors will require renewed belief in yourself and your abilities more than others. The more complex a habit is, the more constituent simpler habits there are in order to achieve it. If a goal seems too monumental, break it down to simple progressive steps: These are the micro habits. (Like writing a paragraph daily.) The effectiveness of micro habits is that when you repeat a small task enough times, it seems natural only to take a bigger step next time, and the whole task no longer looks so intimidating.

Step 2: Be Accountable and Make Use of Push-Pull Reinforcements for Your MicroHabits

In order to create and reinforce new habits, you have to hit both levers of the reptilian brain. To jumpstart the habit, use negative reinforcement as the push. To maintain the momentum, use positive reinforcement as the pull.

Step 3: Use a Trigger

To make the desired positive behavior completely second nature, identify a trigger for the micro habit or the reinforcement process.

The easiest way to guarantee this is to begin with a habit that you already have and then pair it with a microhabit you want to reinforce. For instance, you can use a morning cup of coffee to trigger your writing project micro habit.

Let's look into behavioral habits in detail.

BEHAVIORAL HABITS

Unlike exercise habits or financial habits, behavioral habits are hard to quantify and measure. But in my experience, using the trigger system to influence behavioral habits can lead to massive changes in your life.

Not all behavior is good or bad. Some of it is simply *neutral* — neither good nor bad. What makes a behavior bad is generally our response to the trigger. If we change our response to a better response or no response, we have a better chance to change the outcome in our favor.

In his book *The Success Principles*, Jack Canfield outlines the following formula:

E + R = O
E (Event / Trigger) + R (Response) = O (Outcome)

When it comes to how you react to triggers, you essentially have two very different guiding forces to choose from:

You can either allow your responses to life's triggers to be driven by:
 # Impulse
 # Old/bad habits
 # Doing what's easiest
 # Instant gratification

Or
 # Purpose
 # Intention
 # Thought

Here are a few examples of behavioral habits that can certainly be classified as bad:

1. Being known to have a short temper
2. Making destructive comments about other people
3. Being closed to feedback

Example 1: *Being known to have a short temper*

Let's say you're known to have a short fuse. You want to change that perception. You decide, "I need to control my anger."

What do you do?

Many people don't know where to start. Counting till 10 before speaking, trying to control the anger, treating other people with respect, etc., seems akin to a complete personality change. When you get angry, you are generally out of control. And when you have lost control, you have generally lost the friendship of the other person.

Fortunately, there is a simpler way to get around this problem. Instead of trying to come up with ways to control your anger, simply try to control what you say when you are angry. Or don't speak or react when you are angry. You don't have to change your personality. You don't have to placate people who make you angry or try to get all mystical and convert your negative energy into positive energy. Choose to walk away, or if it is not possible to walk out of the room, simply walk away mentally from that conversation.

The trigger stays the same but you are training yourself to react differently.

All you have to do is...nothing.

When your wife tries to be a backseat driver while you are driving, say nothing.

When someone openly contradicts you in a meeting, quietly consider their point and say nothing.

When your son sneaks your car out for a drive, say nothing, but hide the keys in a better spot. :)

Example 2: *Making destructive comments about other people*

If you have the habit of mouthing off or making destructive comments about other people, you can apply a similar principle to control yourself.

Before making a comment, ask yourself:
#1. Will this comment help the person I'm talking to?
#2. Will this comment help the person I'm talking about?

If the answer is no, don't make that comment! This is easier said than done, but in my own experience, it's totally worth it!

Example 3: *Being closed to feedback*

A lot of us are doing very well in life, and when we take up a challenge, we see it through, but when it comes to our self-improvement, we are sometimes blindsided by problems that we ourselves were not aware of but were obvious to other people.

Some of these problems occur because:
1. We do not know how to recognize the problem;
2. We have not been told about the problem; or
3. We are aware of the problem but refuse to change.

Don't hide from the truth you need to hear. If you are aware of the problem and refuse to change, then there is nothing much this book can do, but if you are open to feedback, you can enhance your relationships, improve your interpersonal skills, and take control of your life. Being open to feedback is the first step before you identify the trigger that is causing the behavioral habit.

Tips for asking for feedback:

1. **Ask the right people.** You would not ask your barber for stock market advice, right? The strange thing about this is that people will often look for feedback from people who will *agree* with them! This is counterproductive. If you don't ask the right people, you will always get information that is biased or irrelevant.

2. **Ask the right questions.** Often, we get the wrong answer because we are asking the wrong question. If you take the time to figure out what the right question is rather than thinking out aloud, you will notice the quality of answers will improve simply because you are asking better questions. A problem well stated is a problem half-solved.

3. **Interpret the answers properly.** Our lives are colored with the lens of our own perceptions and feelings. This part is not easy, because it requires us to consider other perspectives and interpret the meaning of the feedback we receive from the point of view of another person.

4 . **Accept them as accurate.** If you have asked the right people and you are asking the right questions and there is a recurring theme in the feedback, there is no escaping it — don't discredit the messenger or shoot the messenger or get defensive.

In the next chapter, I will introduce a concept attributed to the famous comedian Jerry Seinfeld.

DON'T BREAK THE CHAIN (CHAIN TRACKING)

Chain Tracking as a concept has been attributed to Jerry Seinfeld. The premise is that small daily steps need to be tracked in order to make measurable progress.

Seinfeld realized that in order to be successful, he needed to be consistent. As a comedian, he needed to find ways to write jokes daily. He had a large calendar that showed all the days and months of the year on one page. When he successfully wrote a joke, he marked that day with a large red X, to show that he had accomplished his target. As a result, he would end up having a chain of X's throughout the days and weeks. The more days he wrote jokes, the longer the chain grew. The continuity, or the strength of the chain, is determined by this consistency. If he skipped a single day, he would break the chain.

There might be some days where you might not feel so good, which can affect the consistency of your chain. For that reason, you might be forced to take a different action for the sake of maintaining your chain's consistency.

When you set up a task that seems to be too much to manage, it might lead you to breaking the chain. However, the 1-Minute Habits method can help to ensure your chain grows steadily. This method will work if you have set feasible goals or habits. It is all about achieving them, bit by bit.

The method is super valuable, because it helps you to be more consistent in your efforts. When you are determined to measure your progress and form a long chain, you will be motivated. Consequently, you will disrupt any impulses that might push you to do anything that goes against your plan. Since you will always remember that the chain should not be broken, you will work hard to avoid all the negative actions that might break it.

It is not a must that you have a large calendar to move along with chain tracking. A normal calendar can also work with this method; however, make sure that your X's are big enough. The concept is that X's that are more visible will motivate you and make the chain look larger. You can also opt for calendar chain apps and software, or handmade and printed calendars.

Handmade and Printed Calendars

A large calendar on the wall makes noticeable display, which will be easier to track, and it also acts as a motivator. You might want to hang the calendar in your bedroom, preferably on the wall parallel to your bed. When you place it parallel to your bed, you end up seeing it first thing in the morning. You will also be reminded about the progress of your chain before you sleep. For chain tracking to be successful, you can also print a monthly calendar, which will have bigger X's. However, you can choose yearly calendars, too, according to your preference.

How Long Should Your Chain Be?

This question translates as "how long does it take to develop a particular habit?" Normally, you have a target — maybe a streak of 50 days on your calendar. When you reach the 50th day, it doesn't mean that you should quit. Rather, you can target 60, 70, and so on. Basically, the point here is to challenge yourself on how long the chain can be. There isn't really a limit to the chain's length. You can decide to have a whole-year chain, just for the sake of challenging yourself.

One of the best ways to create a chain reaction in your life is by following a morning routine. Let's understand how to identify triggers for your morning routine.

CHOOSING A TRIGGER FOR YOUR MORNING ROUTINE

The most important aspect of your day's productivity is getting started in the morning. That's why you have to choose your morning triggers with care. Triggers are things that propel you into action, the same way that the starter pistol at the beginning of a race lets the runners know that it's time to move.

Your morning triggers are simply the actions that prompt your habits, such as getting up and brushing your teeth when you get out of bed.

How to Choose Your Triggers

There are a few things to consider when you're selecting your morning routine triggers. For instance:

Your old habits could serve as morning triggers. These old habits are already imprinted on your brain and may still be a part of your daily routine. Your habits could include going to the bathroom at the same time each morning or doing laundry on the same days each week.

Make sure your triggers are easy to remember and execute. If you have to remind yourself of the triggers, this is a sign that they are not effective. Triggers should be automatic and take little to no thought, like the way you automatically make a pot of coffee after brushing your teeth. If you catch yourself forgetting the habit, there is a good chance that you have identified the wrong trigger.

Remember that just about any event or action can serve as a trigger for you. You can use triggers like the end of your favorite newscast or the time you leave for work. As long as it's something that happens every day, the trigger can be effective. Once you notice the triggers you've chosen each day, you should start your morning routine right away. For the first few weeks, you may need to keep a checklist for yourself. After this point, acting as a result of your triggers will be second nature.

Connect Your Triggers to Your Routine

Once you've chosen the trigger you want to use, you need to make a connection between these triggers and your morning routine. For instance, when you hear the newscaster giving the closing remarks on the newscast, this is your sign to set aside about half an hour for your morning chores, like feeding the dogs or taking out the trash. The more you react to the trigger, the more it will become etched in your memory and motivate you to act.

Reduce Your Chances of Failure

When it comes to your morning routine, you are your own worst enemy. Set yourself up for success by making it easier for you to complete your morning tasks. Make sure you're able to do everything on your morning routine list in the shortest amount of time possible.

You can also go to bed early each night so you won't take so long to get out of bed in the mornings. Products, software, or devices like a time management app or electric toothbrush can improve your life and make it easier to help you stick to your morning routine.

If a few days go by and you notice that you're not able to complete everything on your morning to-do list, it's time to make adjustments. Don't put too many things on your list, since this will frustrate you and keep you from sticking to your routine. Edit your morning routine until you can do everything on your list within the allotted time.

Reward Yourself

In order to ensure that you stick to your morning routine, reward yourself when you complete everything on your list. Your "prizes" don't have to be anything too fancy. For instance, you can give yourself a few extra minutes of relaxation time or simply compliment yourself on a job well done. When you get instant gratification, you're making it easier to continue good habits. Breaking the monotony of your morning rituals by celebrating your accomplishments will keep you from getting off of your routine. This will also help your productive habits to stick, which can help with time management and lower your stress levels.

In the next chapter, we will learn about Habit Modification using triggers.

MODIFY YOUR HABITS AND IMPROVE YOUR LIFE

Habits can be your road to success or the key to your downfall. Negative habits are often the toughest ones to let go. So how about changing these negative ones and making them more positive? Changing a habit requires conscious effort and dedication. In some fortunate instances, however, it's not willpower but rather chance that spurs this change.

If your mission is to lose 50 pounds, yet the pastry shop near the office is too tempting, it becomes impossible to accomplish your goals. Who can live without a bite of those mouthwatering pastries? A bite becomes two bites, and then ten. Before you know it, you have gained five pounds more! But if necessity compelled you to switch jobs, placing your pastry shop outside your daily commute zone, you would by default stop indulging in those delicious delicacies. As the days go by, you'd notice you'd lost three pounds without even trying — just because you changed jobs.

Habits and actions have a domino effect. On noticing the trigger, you act upon it and ultimately reward yourself, as is your habit. In this case, the pastry shop was the trigger, walking into the shop was the routine, and the pastry itself became your reward. By removing the trigger, the routine and reward were disconnected from the sequence.

Unfortunately, removing the trigger isn't so simple. It is only sometimes that chance factors interrupt your life to bring about drastic change. Instead, it is hard work to keep temptation at bay. Since habits are unconscious, it requires conscious effort to bring about change. You need to make a plan and have the will to stick to it, no matter how hard it seems.

You do not consciously decide how many spoons of sugar to put in your morning coffee, nor are you aware of biting your nails every time you are nervous. These are things that, if you want to reach a particular goal, might need to be changed. By becoming conscious of the problem, you will be able to consistently avoid acting on it. Through repetition, your altered action will become a habit, instead. It will soon become embedded in your subconscious, thereby changing the bad habit into a positive one. However, since habits are oftentimes formed without knowing, you must re-evaluate them regularly to see if you've picked up any new negative ones.

Making a Plan

The first step toward habit change is acceptance, followed by planning. In order to do this, determine how you want to change your existing habit, how it negatively affects you presently, and what you wish to achieve out of the change. Decide how you wish to achieve this objective and always keep a positive attitude.

Perhaps your goal is to eat healthier. Grab a sheet of paper and write down your plan. Your plan may look something like this:

"I plan on eating healthier food to get a healthier body. For this, I will avoid eating cookies daily. Instead, I will try to eat fruits and vegetables. I will not forget to take my vitamins, and moreover, I will also exercise regularly. By doing so, I will feel better and have more energy and increased stamina. This will help me accomplish more work, play with my children, and feel happier overall."

This outline becomes a future vision for yourself. Go one step further and envision this with all your heart and will. If you are aware of the *New York Times* Bestseller, *The Secret*, you already know what to do. The Law of Attraction says it all: By envisioning a future and willing it, you will be able to achieve it.

Famous personalities such as Oprah Winfrey are followers of the Law of Attraction, and they have recommended using a vision board. Instead of simply envisioning your goals in your mind, place them in front of you. It may be a whiteboard, a corner of the wall, or even a refrigerator where you place specific items, phrases, or anything that helps you focus on your goal. If your goal is to stop nail biting, put up pictures of beautiful nails, thereby reminding yourself of your ultimate aim. By seeing this every day, you will feel increasingly encouraged to achieve it.

Tracking Habits

Even as you are trying to make a change, try keeping a journal to record the negative habit. Take for example that you want to stop drinking too much coffee. Record every cup of coffee with a note in a journal or a smartphone. You will need to make multiple columns to keep careful tabs of your habit.

An example of the column titles and what such a journal entry may look like is shown below:

Date and Time: Tuesday, 15th March, 10:23am
Emotional State Before the Behavior: Very sleepy and stressed
Physical State Before the Behavior: At the café outside the office
Frequency and Duration of the Behavior: 2 cups of coffee so far
Emotional State After Behavior: Relaxed and wide awake.

As you try hard to make a change, within a week you may notice a shift in its frequency. By noting the trigger, sleepiness and stress in this case, you can begin thinking about a good method for replacing the behavior with a more acceptable behavior.

Set Goals

Both long-term and short-term goals are essential, apart from the vision. Perhaps your long-term goal is to lose 50 pounds and keep that weight off. You may also add goals such as "reduced cholesterol levels" and "reduced blood pressure" to this list. But this may not be achievable in a single shot.

Instead, set short-term and middle-term goals, such as losing 10 pounds in two weeks and 20 pounds by the end of the month. Take it one step at a time, and before long, you will have reached the finish line. By setting short-term goals, your final aim does not look like an overwhelming and impossible achievement. Instead, it reminds you that everything is still possible.

To remind yourself of your progress, write the goals on paper and check them off as you slowly begin achieving them. Every tick will add to your confidence, taking you one step closer to the final result.

Believe and Commit

While commitment is essential for the success of any plan, belief is equally important. If you remain uncertain, constantly in doubt, and question yourself on your success, chances are you will give up. The commitment that you promised might end up in a relapse as you decide you cannot achieve your goal, that it feels impossible.

Believe in yourself, because otherwise, you can do nothing. Have faith in your ability to reach that goal; only then will you be able to fully commit to achieving it. Psychologists have proven that believing is a key factor in success, and the vision board mentioned earlier will help instill just that within you.

Remember: Habits never die as long as the trigger is present

Much like learning to ride a bike, a habit, once formed, is never forgotten. It cannot be lost, for it becomes embedded in your subconscious. However, you can change it. Try altering the habit to accommodate your life and your goals, using it to your advantage. You may want to continue biting your nails when nervousness strikes, but instead, occupy your fingers with something else. Perhaps twirling your hair, or writing out why you are nervous.

Old habits are harder to break, so try to catch them early on. If you notice that every time you get upset or happy, you tend to shop, you may be forming a shopping addiction. Stop it before it gets worse. Channel your shopping energy into something else before you are plunged into a mountain of credit card debt.

Remember that habits, even the ones that have been overcome, have the power to resurface. By introducing the previous triggers and stimuli, an ex-smoker may still pick up a cigarette and plunge headlong into this negative habit all over again. In order to maintain the transformed habit, you need to be aware of your triggers!

While smoking is more of an addition rather than a habit — the principles for tackling this addiction are essentially the same — let us look into how we can swap out bad habits for good ones.

HABIT SWAPPING

If you plan on moving past your negative behavior, then you need to learn how to replace bad habits with good habits. We've seen that rerouting behavior can be easily done by recognizing the triggers, yet we've also seen that it's essential to find a new behavior to follow that trigger up with.

Eliminating a trigger, though, can be a bit complicated, since most of the times it's something really normal, such as a need for comfort, being tired, feeling upset, or even being with someone in a certain place. However, there is something you can do, and that's change the way you respond to triggers. To do that, you need to learn how to swap negative habits for positive ones.

First of all, it's important that you decide whether you want to go for a total or partial swap, which may be increased over time. This generally depends on your personality and your habit, so make sure that you're completely honest with yourself and whether you can manage swapping habits.

Swap Like for Like

To be really honest, there are no real wrong or right swaps, but it's recommended that you go mostly for those swaps that seem logical to you. So for instance, if you want to break the habit of eating candy because it's not good for your health, it's going to be a lot easier to replace it with sunflower seeds than going for a jog around the block.

If you want to successfully swap a negative habit for a positive one, then you need to make sure that the latter makes you feel rewarded. If it doesn't, then it'll simply not work and you'll return to your old negative habits very soon. Therefore, make sure you don't swap eating candy with eating vegetables, especially if you hate them. Instead, choose a healthy snack replacement that makes you feel rewarded and one that you genuinely like.

What is My Reward?

Below, you can find some great examples of positive swaps and the many rewards they provide. You can even consider using some of them if you are out of ideas:

If you really want to quit smoking, but have no idea what to replace it with, then how about replacing it with exercising? The good news about exercising is that not only does it help you look better, but it also improves your health greatly. You're basically getting instant health benefits and a distraction from the habit of smoking. Regardless if it's a lap at the local swimming pool, a jog around the lake, or some cardio, exercising improves your health and also makes for a perfect habit replacement that can easily help you forget all about smoking.

When it comes to food swaps, most people think about taste, but they forget about a very important detail — the texture of the food. This means you actually may not be addicted to the potato chips themselves, but their crunch. As an alternative, you should consider other crunchy snacks, such as popcorn, crackers, or nuts. One very important detail to keep in mind is that unhealthy foods should always be swapped with healthier options, since this is an essential part of the habit-breaking process.

At the end of the day, it's very important that you try as much as possible to identify your triggers and swap negative behaviors with positive ones. By incorporating a reward system in your swap, you'll easily be able to get rid of negative behaviors, increase your self-esteem, and finally regain control over your life.

Creating habit barriers

If all this does not help you shed bad habits, create barriers to the trigger. So, perhaps you have a fetish for eating ice cream every night and always keep some in your freezer. You will never stop the habit if the ice cream is there. Its temptation is too great; just don't buy ice-cream.

It's easier for you to avoid ice cream if there's none there.

Suppose your fetish is so strong that you are ready to head to the store to buy some. Have your spouse hide your car keys. This way, you have to ask for them to go out. Inform your spouse about your attempts at kicking the ice cream habit. Tell him or her not to give you the keys if you are heading to the ice cream shop. (Similarly, shopaholics, don't go shopping if you don't want to spend money.)

You need to avoid places that indulge the habit to stop it. Spend more time with people who are against the habit. You could apply transparent nail polish to your nails to stop biting your nails. Or you can take Antabuse, the drug that makes alcoholics feel sick when they drink alcohol.

Different environment

Besides all these habit-changing methods, you can also try changing your environment. Most habits are triggered by your environment; changing it can help you avoid your habit. If you want to stop smoking, and tend to smoke with beer, avoid beer. Replace it with a drink that does not make you smoke. If you chew tobacco with certain friends at a baseball game, but not with your wife, go to games with your wife or other friends who don't chew tobacco.

Changing your environment doesn't have to mean moving into a new house or quitting your job (though it certainly could mean that). It might just mean moving that chair where you sit and smoke off the patio, or not keeping sweets in the house. It could mean moving your television so that you can't see it from the table where you eat dinner because you don't want the family to watch TV while they eat. Changing your environment can also mean not hanging out with people who share, and thus encourage, your bad habits.

In the next chapter, we will try to examine the root causes— in other words, finding the WHY behind some common habits.

FINDING THE WHY

Once you have established what your habits are and are starting to identify the triggers that set these habits off, the next step is to work out why they have become your habits. We form habits for a reason, and understanding these reasons can be the key to getting rid of the habit.

Habits can be good or bad, but what you need to understand is what triggers these habits. Only after understanding your habits and what makes you behave in a certain manner will you be able to get rid of the habit.

Below is a detailed analysis of some of the causes of your habits and how they affect your life.

Comfort: Different people find comfort in different activities, and you might be amazed by the unusual behaviors in which people find comfort. Sometimes, these habits emerge from psychological issues that were not addressed in childhood and the feeling of nostalgia that comes back at times to affect you later in life. Whether you like biting your nails, eating certain foods, or listening to a certain type of music to make you feel good, you need to understand the reasons behind that behavior. As much we may try hard to quit certain habits, it becomes impossible to stop every time.

Social Influence: Regardless of age, we are all greatly influenced by our peers. A sense of belonging and the need to feel accepted by those you interact with can lead you into engaging in certain activities unwillingly. Whether at school, home, or work, we all try to impress others, either to look cool or to fit in so that we do not get left out of social activities. As a result, you find kids and even adults engaging in heavy drinking, drug abuse, or other activities that eventually become habits. Making independent decisions does not mean that you will automatically quit the habit, but it is a crucial first step.

Inherited Habits: In most cases, people tend to carry on habits they've inherited — not genetically, but by learning and imitation. Both children and adults have role models they look up to with respect and admiration. When we are young, our parents and other people around us have a great impact in shaping our behavior in the future. Children learn through imitating behavior, and if you grew up observing certain habits from your role models, there is a high probability that you will take up these habits.

Avoidance: We are all human, and we face day-to-day challenges that take a toll on us. Feelings of anxiety and depression may lead to you to certain decisions that provide immediate gratification to escape from reality. Similarly, the challenges of life may make you start doing things that become habitual slowly and gradually. Maybe you are short on confidence; a little alcohol gives you false high esteem and you are able to do anything when high. In the end, you may find that you cannot undertake any demanding or challenging activity without first having a glass of wine, and it ends up becoming a habit.

Poor Lifestyle Choices: Some choices we make in life lead to other consequences that need to be addressed. In trying to cope with the effects of a certain behavior, you may end up developing a certain habit to compensate for your actions. For example, if you used to party a lot in college, you may have had to consume an energy drink every morning before attending classes so you had the energy to get through the day. As this became a repeated behavior, you found yourself in a position where you could not stop drinking an energy drink every morning. Although you may not be entirely dependent on the drink, the fact you are used to it means that without it, you feel incomplete.

Whatever your habit, finding the root cause can be as simple as thinking it through or as complex as speaking to a parent or someone else who has known you a long time and really soul-searching to find the cause. This can be an emotional process.

To help you get to the root cause of a habit, ask yourself the following questions:

How does it make me feel? If you feel comforted, happy, or reassured by the habit, ask yourself, is this happiness long-lasting and free from a downside? For example, it feels lovely to eat cake, but the pleasure is usually momentary, the health impact is negative, and the feeling afterward when a healthy eating plan has been sabotaged can be really horrible. Ask yourself why you need that sense of comfort in your life, and look at when it started to represent comfort and happiness to you. Was there a particular time when you felt like you had to engage in this habit to "treat" yourself or to undo negative feelings? Why did this continue to the present day? Do you still need this comfort, or could you make it redundant now that it is no longer needed?

You might find that doing the habitual doesn't actually make you feel good anymore. This is a fantastic realization, because it means that you can free yourself from the feeling that you "need" to do the habitual activity and can move past it knowing that it is no longer required.

Is it really *my* habit? Ask yourself if this habit is all you, or if it is a habit you have developed as a response to another person or group of people. You might be surprised to find that your habit is one you share with a parent or with a teacher, friend, or other influential person. If you see someone engage in a habit often enough, you may find yourself copying the behavior without realizing you are doing it, or you may feel that imitating this person helps you to feel that you are like them in some way. That's why you are more likely to find that you have inherited a habit from someone you respect. Figure out what attribute you most admired or desired in this person and you may realize that you have moved on and no longer see them as a role model. At the very least, you may understand that their habits, like yours, are just habits and have nothing to do with what you respect or admire them for.

Where does the pressure come from? If you feel pressure to continue with a habit, work out where it is coming from. Added pressure can come from other people around you who engage in the same habit (for example, smoking cigarettes). Other pressure can come from stressful situations; many habits are a response to anxiety. Additional pressure can come from a busy lifestyle — you may feel you don't have time to devote to quitting the habit. At times, your habit provides you with an excuse to step outside your routine and have a few moments to yourself; for example, you might end up drinking too much caffeine because a coffee means a short break from work. Knowing where the pressure to continue the habitual behavior comes from can be one of the crucial keys to breaking your sense of dependency on your habit. Feeling free from this pressure will always feel better than the habit itself can make you feel.

Final Analysis

Whatever your habit is, you need to ask yourself the following questions: Does it make you feel good? If it does, does it have long-term benefits? Is it a habit that you actually love? Where does the pressure to do this thing come from? After this, you will realize that the solution to quitting the habit could be as simple as self-analysis and meditation or talking to someone close to you.

In the next chapter, we will learn how to avoid some common habit triggers.

HOW TO AVOID HABIT TRIGGERS

You can identify your habit triggers when they occur and stop them before anything bad happens. This can be possible when you realize your habit, where it came from, and what triggered it.

Realizing Your Habit Triggers

The first thing here is to actually understand your habits, together with their triggers. In order to successfully identify the habit and its triggers, you will need to be consistent. As you are trying to work on the old triggers of your habits, some new triggers can develop in the process.

The Internal and External Triggers

Generally, habit triggers can be split into two categories: internal and external triggers. Your triggers can fall into either of the two or, in most cases, into both categories. Normally, external triggers lead to internal triggers, which in turn lead to a behavior.

The internal triggers are those that occur in you

devoid of any external incitement. You might be used to getting up early in the morning, even if you are not supposed to go anywhere. This could be because you used to wake up very early in the morning to study for school many years ago. This will now become a habitual behavior, which comes from within.

The external triggers are those things that occur for the sake of stimulating your habitual behavior. These triggers can be stuff like bad news, which may lead you to pull out your hair. It may also be a certain place that affects your behavior.

Evading the Habit Triggers

Sometimes you can completely avoid a trigger, and at other times you can avoid it partially. Being mindful about your triggers is what matters most, so you need to be aware of that. For instance, if you tend to smoke when you are bored, then you can try to be occupied to avoid boredom.

The trick of avoiding your triggers is disrupting a trigger that may stimulate you to do something habitual. Tackling the reason behind the habit will help you to avoid the habit. The process involves identifying the problem — when it happened, the reaction, what you felt and the triggers. After understanding the triggers, you'll then need to find ways of avoiding them when they occur.

Tips on How to Deal with Your Habit Triggers

#1. *Identify the Trigger*: The first thing here is to recognize the habit triggers, which will prove that you are successful with the mindfulness process. Identifying the trigger also helps you to know how to deal with it, so as to avoid it the next time.

#2. *Disrupt the Trigger*: After you have recognized the trigger, you will now need to take immediate actions to sabotage it. If you delay, the habitual behavior might take root for the long run. The faster you can disrupt the trigger, the more likely you are to avoid the habitual behavior.

#3. *Come up with an Alternative*: In case you end up engaging in your habitual behavior, you can find alternatives to deal with the situation. Identify what happened, why it happened and find ways of dealing with the habit trigger better next time. Even though you ended up engaging in the habitual behavior, you can be sure of being closer to avoiding it next time if you find an alternative ahead of time.

#4. *Encourage Yourself on Your Achievements*: When you manage to disrupt the habit trigger and successfully avoid the habitual behavior, you should be happy and record your progress. You can note down what happened, what you did about it, and why it was successful.

#5. *Repeat the Process*: The key to countering the triggers is by being consistent. For that, you should repeat the entire trigger evasion progress. This will make it easier, and you will naturally know when a trigger can occur and deal with it before it leads to a habit.

Repetition is key to incorporating new habits. In the next chapter, we will examine how to create a routine to install new habits.

ALL YOU NEED TO KNOW ABOUT MAKING OR BREAKING A HABIT

Before you ingrain a habit into your daily life, it must undergo a phase of repetition. Let us take the example of a child who is just learning to walk. The child takes time to understand many things, like shifting her body weight from one foot to another, positioning the feet and maintaining her body's balance. Whenever when she wobbles dangerously in the room, you can't help but wonder if she is going to fall. Suddenly, you will see her beginning to walk, then run and even hop around.

So, what do we understand from this? The more you keep trying to do something, the less wobbly your steps become.

This principle of repetition applies even for breaking a habit. William James, the father of American psychology, made a detailed study on repetition and how our minds are affected by it. A new activity may be done with difficulty for the first time, but soon it can be done with ease. Finally, you reach a state where you will be able to perform it while hardly being conscious about it. James explains it beautifully by comparing it with a sheet of paper, which upon folding tends to retain the folds or creases.

The actual time needed for breaking a habit depends on the following factors:

#1. What is the motivation behind your urge to change? Habits affecting your health are easier to break compared to ones having less negative impact on your life.

#2. What is the nature of the habit? Does it involve emotional reliance or physical dependence?

#3. For how long have you had the habit?

#4. Do you have any support from others to break the habit?

#5. How strong is your personality? Are you self-confident, or do you suffer from low self-esteem? Do you have determination, or lack willpower?

Likewise, the duration for establishing a new habit is also based on several aspects:

#1. The habit's complexity. Is it a simple habit, like brushing your teeth before going to bed, or does it #2. need you to make a major lifestyle change?

#3. How often will you have to reinforce the habit — weekly, daily or hourly?

#4. How determined you are to inculcate the habit? Are you really excited about it?

#5. Can you get the support of your family or friends?

Step 1: Define a Timeline

It is critical to emphasize the timeline you define will not provide a deadline for mastering your new habits. The overused statement, "It takes 21 days to develop a new habit," is a myth based upon debunked research conducted by NASA. (For more information, see: http://www.7bigrocks.com/productivity/habits/debunking-the-21-day-habit-forming-myth/). You do not know how long it will take for you to develop a new habit, so putting a deadline on your progress will give your mind a target to shoot for.

The key aspect of a timeline is to focus on the present. You can never live in the future or the past; you can only live in the present. The timeline that you need to implement is determining when you will review your progress and struggles. It is a commitment, with concrete times to hold yourself accountable. Give yourself time to see progress or failure so you can be either inspired by your dedication to achieving a goal or use good anger to overcome the bondage of a bad habit.

Step 2: Keep a Journal

A journal is potentially your most important tool in changing your habits. Depending on how you use it, your journal will be a window into your mind and how it perceives change. This doesn't mean you need to spend hours on end detailing every minute of the day. Instead, keep track of your timeline and log whether you felt successful or unsuccessful in the accountability check. Write a few sentences describing your feelings and what positive coping skills you used to remain in the present. A well-developed journal entry will provide you with a reference tool, a way to stay in the present, an opportunity to vent, and a look back at your gradual success in changing habits.

I wish that I could say that identifying triggers and swapping out habits has always worked for me — the fact is that it hasn't — so let me share what you can do when you experience setbacks.

HANDLING SETBACKS

It is wise to perceive setbacks as unavoidable circumstances, because with such a perception you can come up with an emergency plan for how to handle them. Discussed below is a plan of five steps for dealing with setbacks in case they occur in the process of quitting a habit.

Admit You Slid Back

Sometimes, it's easy to fall back into an old habit when you are trying to start a new one. If it happens, do not deny that fact. Admit it happened as soon as it does and stop it immediately. This way, you will reverse the effects of your mistake and reduce the amount of harm the setback could do to your determination and confidence to quit.

For instance, you can be a habitual sugar eater who has decided to quit the habit, but somehow you find yourself eating a sugar-laden bar of chocolate. Once you realize your mistake, stop eating the bar immediately. If your goal is to quit smoking, once you buy a packet of cigarettes and realize your mistake after smoking one cigarette, do not finish off the packet. Instead, stop at that one cigarette and focus on quitting the habit. Record why you slipped back, as this will help you to identify the trigger hence avoid future setbacks.

Avoid Beating Yourself Up

Setbacks don't necessarily mean that you are a failure or a loser in breaking a habit. It just means you are human. Stopping a bad habit is a process, which means it might not be smooth all the way. Do not be too harsh on yourself. To curb future setbacks, record why you slipped up and how you intend to avoid a repetition of the habitual behavior.

In some cases, the setback might be as a result of an unplanned-for situation, and so you can forgive yourself for running to the unwanted habit for comfort or consolation. However, having gone through the situation, make a plan for how to deal with related risks and get rid of the bad habit.

Start Anew

After a setback, it is likely that you feel less confident and less motivated to change your habit. Try to pick yourself up, renew your commitment, and decide to start anew with fresh energy. For instance, you may sign up for a new exercise class to replace a bad habit or find new recipes in case you want to replace a bad eating habit with a healthy eating habit. These new changes will excite you and inspire you to continue making the necessary habitual changes. In other words, find new ideas and methods to help you get motivated to achieve your goal.

When starting a new habit, adopt a positive attitude, because it will help you to forge a way forward even when things seem tough on you. Every setback informs you of your weaknesses and therefore teaches you who you are and how you can avoid them in future.

The "one step at a time" approach will make it easier for you to change your habit. The change may seem like a big burden or responsibility when you look at it in its entirety, but when you perceive it as a single step at a time, you are better off.

To grasp the one-step-at-a-time approach, here is a breakdown:

1st Step: Awareness. Aspire to always be alert of whatever it is you are doing. Bad decisions are made when you allow yourself to be unaware of your habits.

2nd Step: Always think of an option, a Plan B. When you are aware or alert, you will not forget that you have an option to behave otherwise. How you behave is your choice.

3rd Step: Trust the option you go with. The knowledge that you have the power to choose your habits should help you to trust yourself to opt for the right decision.

4th Step: Whatever decision you make, own it!

Accepting your decisions to behave in a certain manner, whether good or bad, is a big step in admitting that you are human. If there is something you can do about a setback to change your habit, do it, but if you can't, learn your lesson and focus on your future decisions on your habit.

5th Step: Focus on the future. When one moment passes, another one begins. Such is life. You should therefore make a constant decision to move forward. Live the present moment and continue focusing on the future change of habit.

As an action plan, in the next two days, practice the one-step-at-a-time approach and write a journal about the decisions you had to make concerning your habit and the ones you made.

Read on for a quick three-step plan to help you get started right away.

CONCLUSION

Bad habits lead us in the opposite direction from our goals. They lead to more stress, less satisfaction, more frustration, and less fulfillment. The truth is that no matter how much willpower you have, a habit cannot be broken so long as the trigger is present.

You've now learned the entire system — what it is, why it works, and how it works. Now, it's time to put it to use in your own life and business.

To help get you up and running quickly, here's a simple three-step action plan:

Step 1: Grab a pen and paper and note down your bad habits for each of the following areas.

#1. Your health, food, and exercise
#2. How you start and end your workday
#3. Your urges

#4. Your unproductive activities

#5. How you manage your emotional responses

#6. How you spend your money

#7. Things you procrastinate on that you know you really should be doing

Step 2: Identify and write down the triggers for each of these bad habits. Also write down the replacement habit you will swap the bad habit with, while ensuring that the trigger stays the same. If you are unable to come up with ideas for replacement habits, a quick Internet search will help you get additional ideas and come up with strategies to counter your bad habits.

Step 3: Every week, choose one bad habit that you want to change. At the end of the year, you will have eliminated 52 bad habits from your life!

Now you are equipped with all the tools to swap out your bad habits with good ones. Keep or replace any of the methods as you see fit. Just remember that the overall goal is to keep things moving so it does not get too monotonous.

There may be setbacks, but there are also solutions to the problems that arise. With some dedication, motivation and a good understanding of what habits are and why they happen, any unwanted habit can be replaced with something more positive that enables you to take control of your life.

I wish you all the best in your life journey. Don't forget to collect your free gift on the next page.
:)

YOUR FREE GIFT

As a way of saying, "Thanks for your purchase," I'm offering a free download of my ebook "Wake Up Successful - How to Increase Your Energy & Achieve Any Goal with a Morning Routine".

Getting Unstuck is a real problem for a lot of people. The trick is to identify what you need to get done and create a step-by-step strategy to launch your day so that you execute your tasks in the most efficient way possible.

In "Wake Up Successful" you'll discover several ways to launch your day with a tried and tested morning routine. This will enable you to make lasting changes to your work, success, health and sleep habits.

You can download this free ebook by clicking here

http://7bigrocks.com/mr/

http://7bigrocks.com/mr/

CPSIA information can be obtained at www.ICGtesting.com
Printed in the USA
LVOW06s2345100815

449560LV00033B/1920/P